WRECKS

Wve

ERIN L. McCOY

ecks

ISBN 978-1-955992-63-3

PUBLISHED BY NOEMI PRESS, INC.
A NONPROFIT LITERARY ORGANIZATION
WWW.NOEMIPRESS.ORG

COVER AND INTERIOR DESIGN
BY ALBAN FISCHER

Contents

FIGURES

The great auk was a flightless seabird, found only in the North Atlantic, that stood about thirty inches tall and looked not unlike a penguin, except for its small, bent wings, similar to a flying bird's. Auks were hunted widely for their feathers, eggs, meat, stomachs, fat, and, finally, for trophies of a creature known to be increasingly rare.

The last two confirmed members of the species were killed in 1844 off the coast of Iceland, on an island called Eldey. The extinction of the great auk helped contribute to a growing awareness of humans' role in extinction events.

The auk was repeatedly described by those who encountered the bird as making human-like gestures and sounds, including sighs. One of the last recorded auks was killed in 1840 by three St. Kildan sailors who became convinced over the course of three days—during which they were stranded by bad weather—that the auk was a witch and was causing the storm.

White whales

Water can disguise itself: chapped
lips, gnawed tundra, or the glass
stomach of an abyssal fish with still-

burning mammoths inside it.
In captivity one auk liked to flaunt
her swimming at the end of a rope.

With winter's approach, white feathers
bloomed at her neck. She slipped off;
soon rumors of a body limp ashore

at Gourock; how to know except
to cut her open, plumb the gut
for hemp fiber and milk? Am I just

another thief? Have I taken her blood
for my blood instead of bleeding?
A pet is a costume for a feeling—

shifts according to need, like water.
Where anything is forgiven, there's
no need for mercy. I can twist any

crime into a fateful error
till everything's a child's drawing:
house, barn, horse, cross, terror.

Exhibit A: Eldey Island, Iceland, 1844

Squint, reader, through the sudden fog:
                    the sea's gnaw and lick-bright:
Eldey, pillar of stone: where two
                    great auks survive, briefly—
before reenacting the end of their story

                    especially for us. See them flee
the stalking sailor Sigurðr. I, tourist,
                    slip inside his body,
drenched numb by the ice-stout flumes.
                    Cash-sack-fat birds, necks

like liquid: yes—I want to—
                    but the auks' panicked eyes;
tuft of lavender down plucked
                    loose. *It walked like a man*,
Sigurðr will tell later. *He made no cry*.

                    I soak through. I watch
the auks run. He/it and she/it
                    toddle toward the breakers,
the careful steps of children
                    new to all the earth:

Sigurðr's daughter
                    shushing dolls in the haylight.
Or child-me, hiding my witch-heart
                    in a bathroom stall.
By the neck and he flapped his wings.

Sigurðr lifts it in his fist. I lift
him in my fist. We lift her

in our fist. You must believe me—
                    I tried to protect her
when I did not hate her for her failure
                    to be strong.

The auk sighs. The seas pause.
Sigurðr's daughter falls into a deep sleep.

Uncanny valley

Pink millions of passenger pigeons slammed the sun shut again and again for fifty thousand years. Above the Ohio River, a solar eclipse for three days straight as one flock passed over. Men and boys stood on the banks, Audubon wrote, *shooting at the pilgrims*. Who wound down the paved streets, candle-guided in the noon dim. Who believed the devil flew above in sky-wide skeins pinned with ruby eyes. Three days: they claimed they could not take it. Claimed some things were not made for this world. Cast into shade, the city looked different. Like a place where bullets, shot, just disappeared.

◁

The last Pyrenean ibex, Celia, was tracked by radio collar and found at last crushed beneath a fallen trunk. *Gently curved horns.* After three years, fifty-seven implantations, and seven pregnancies, her clone was sliced from a host goat's belly. She couldn't breathe. The theory of relativity states that a life ten minutes long feels as long as any. The woolly mammoth, the great auk, the heath hen, the passenger pigeon are all candidates for de-extinction. Blood down a vein: now open for patent.

◁

If the meal were the whole weight of milk. The udder and the ever-soft calf's tongue. But the meal is a flourish of pigeons cut out of the sky like a bleeding dawn.

If the meal were the heft of whole milk, it could coat your stomach. You could weigh its loss like you drag your own feet. But pigeons sliced from so much, they must be God Himself—you cannot call wanting.

Later, three days become three birds. You remember the underparts of their wings, soft like newborns.

◁

The Second Coming: all ten minutes of gasping It.

◁

Next, wounds miraculously heal. Next, the dead with heads on ice start to speak. And you are ergo pardoned for having not murdered who has been brought back to life, who was wounded only. And the revived heads will co-host parties with the clones of the last-dead members of each species, who have inherited the traits that got them knocked off in the first place: flightlessness, flying too much, being caught between excesses. But by then it is a kinder world. Every tree will be hung with peaches and every night a fresh chilling air. The streamers and cups will be picked up later. They'll send a shiver through you then, though you won't know why.

“Occurrence of a Foreign Bat in Orkney”

After a paper by John Wolley, egg collector and auk researcher, published in Zoologist *in 1849*

There is no explanation for loss. A shovel’s nose smacks the dirt. While digging potatoes, they caught a bat. Band of yellow hair.

On his first trip north, Wolley tracked sea eagles by the lamb-shaped gaps in flocks. A hundred years later, sheep were stamped with bright spots, hot pink or oyster blue or mauve on the haunch. No fear of eagles, long since wiped out.

No such bat lived in all of Scotland. A singularity is lonely; that is its defining fault.

Wolley became worried for the auk. Its shrunken wings were brilliant if observed through the plate glass of the sea’s surface, but on land—a failure of foresight.

Twelve years later, Wolley died at thirty-six. The consensus among the society of the *Ibis* journal is that his brain, like an egg, opened.

There is no explanation for a bird that once could fly and now cannot.

There was little wanting in him, wrote Alfred Newton after Wolley’s death. At the eagle’s reintroduction, sheep flocks fled along the upper slopes of the Orkneys and the Isle of Skye, where the clouds push so near you can stick out your tongue and taste a dozen kinds of snow. North enough that the crevice between heaven and earth is narrow. There’s no use for flight. Pieces of the closest planets used to break off and nest in the crown of the auk’s head.

The motions

Peel my palms apart:
oily aftermath of pretend
prayer. I did what I was told.
I knelt and made motions. Likewise,
when X asked what I saw I said *visions.*
Y said to be loved, you cannot impose.
The story goes that a storm shut its fist
around a one-roomed hut,
caged one auk and three sailors
inside the same exhibit. This
made the sailors squirm.
When they heard the bird
not chirp but muster incantations
—like a witch, they said, [in]human—
saw the whites of her eyes
turn inside their own intelligence,
what could you expect?
Z said I got what I deserved
for my words always swerved in the wrong
directions, burned little fits
and holes into my hosts. So I fell on my knees,
invoked their god whom I could not
feel, beat my lungs clean,
smashed ants with my thumbs, stapled fur onto
fur, pointed,
disappeared into pointing. Sliced
the soles of my feet,
the only skin
no one can see.
Meanwhile, in secret, slipped off
my socks, squirmed on the earth,

took wild strawberries into my
mouth without the aid of fingers.
The auk dozed beside me in the grass
till they came down with stones.
No worse than my crime: I did not want to live
even as she ascended
against her will
through their invention.

auk in the afterlife

the first thing the auk notices about heaven

is just how thin it is: one aglow tentacle
of a jellyfish stretched between the high cirrus

& plankton-dusted space. the amenities are

that it feels like flying & that there's no shade.
the auk is not impressed. she never needed air to fly

& she'd like to sleep without the sun's insistence.

oh well. she bides her time laying eggs on the backs
of passing birds. she dives for plankton but the stars

are farther than they look. space is barren, shorn

only rarely by mute mirror-sided whales. she floats
for some immeasurable period on the tufts of a great

conversion: the sailors of st. kilda, christian at long last.

then they forget what they've done or they die or the wind
changes. the auk, who has subsisted on clouds,

snags a piece of the tastiest & drags it down with her

as she descends. it is then—in how the fogs wreathe her,
in some gone-grey twist of the light—that she

transforms / witch-auk lands in the north atlantic.

she is an invention: the fantasy & its rejection—
a monstrosity—slippage—not-human &

not-not. the sea is a sheet of glass that breaks

to pieces, breaks to pieces—wounds that suture
themselves. working as fast as they can.

Catalog of sunken islands

"Great is the power of the Prince of Darkness."
—S. Thorarinsson in 1950, on Hekla volcano's eruption, 1104 C.E.

1783: BLINDEFUGLASKER ISLAND SINKS
28 MILES OFF THE COAST OF ICELAND

With the eruption of Skaptar-Jokull, thousands in Iceland dead. Crops speckled and brown from sulfuric acid. *[S]tarved and poisoned animals died by thousands.* A grandmother and granddaughter survived winter eating the skin off a sealskin boat.

Blindefuglasker Island, an auk rookery on the rim of an ancient crater, sank into the sea. The eggs sank with it.

Ben Franklin, ambassador to France, found the summer sun so diminished that *when collected in the focus of a burning glass*, its rays *would scarce kindle brown paper.*

1830–1831: GEIRFUGLASKER ISLAND SINKS 26 MILES OFF THE ICELAND COAST

From the closest lighthouse, Geirfuglasker looked *just like Zoega's wide-awake hat.* When asked if they would go to raid eggs, an Icelander said *never, never, never.*

Rhymed a Lutheran pastor:
I have never trusted myself to go to Geirfuglasker,
As, on account of the surf, boats were broken by the waves there.

One man, Thorwaldur, survived there a whole winter, but he wouldn't say how. The following summer, a baby and cradle appeared at the church door at Hvalness. Red coverlet; charred fingers. None would baptize it.

When Geirfuglasker sank, disoriented auks washed ashore on Eldey, a skerry nine miles off the coast—easier to reach than the sunken rookeries had been. One auk was loaded on a ship to France. When she died, she was stuffed and mounted. This auk is today in Nantes.

Thorwaldur years later threw himself into the sea. He became a whale.

Eldey, "the Mealsack." After the first raid, a fishwife skinned twenty-three auks. One was still alive. Hazel eyes, she said.

1844: TUANAKI ISLAND SINKS ~200 MILES SOUTH OF RAROTONGA

While the last two auks were strangled on Eldey, Tuanaki in the southern Cook Islands suddenly could not be found. Whalers once revictualed there, and mission ships with their hulls full of limes.

A sailor who'd visited the reef-linked lagoons, shallows green and slick as taro leaves, reported that Tuanaki was thickly inhabited. *We do not kill men*, a chief told him.

One dusk, a whaling ship dragging Thorwaldur's bloated body moored at Tuanaki. They feasted—burned his fat flanks for days and days, and nights and nights.

The researcher (2020) dreams of Shanawdithit (1828)

Shanawdithit was one of the Beothuk people, who lived in what is now called Newfoundland. The Beothuk traveled to Funk Island in the summers to gather great auks and their eggs for food. Evidence indicates that they may have looked to seabirds as guides to help the dead travel to an island in the west.

When I sleep, you dream, turning and turning
on a soft earth.

Light drools down, blinds me. I can't see your cheek
curve. Words rise

to your lips, tin char to a lake's surface.
I can't hear them.

Shut my eyes, and the brittle birches clank
and squeal above.

That sound is the only thing we have both
touched. Porous

like the edge of sleep. Not like the men sawing,
sawing, who take us

in their holy hold. Who slice down trees to build
crosses, emblems

of their sliced-down lord. I am trying, but I can't pull you
through the breach, while you—

you saved everyone: drew the shapes of their motion:
carved staffs, a cup

your father held. Here we are now, inside my translations
of your translations—

a rendition of loss, of my failure to render.
Am I fooling myself,

that through so much static, I can almost glimpse:

: : : : : : : : : : : : : : : : : : :

:   :   :   :

:   :

:

:

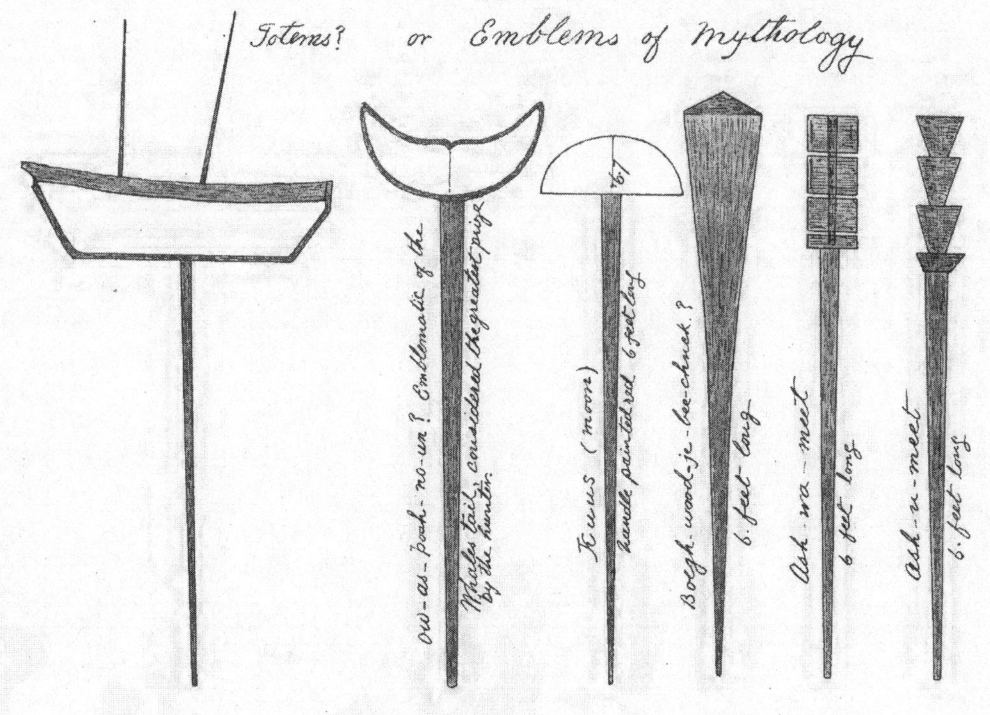

Drawing by Shanawdithit, c. 1828

post-atlantic

after she escapes the sky, witch-auk drifts a long time on an empty atlantic. she washes ashore in new england, & i come to meet her there. down the boardwalk a team of gulls hacks up french fries & steamed clams. one is nutcracker-postured with an entire corndog down his throat; the stick flagpoles out his beak. but look,

the ocean always clung to its bounty. unpalatable fish float inert & crooked like boomerangs, the crabs oily in their mood-ring shells. & that there was once a wild-eyed captain who hunted a single whale for years

isn't that impressive, when others made quicker work of the beasts. a clot of boys at the end of the dock smears us up & down with yellow eyes. they flick their kershaws open & shut. i let them crack me open, cut out & examine my organs one by one—no pearl, disappointment—toss them off the pier. witch-auk presses her cheek into my palm. when

will she find out about me? a drunk man toddles up to us, says his name is gary, tells us his story, how he's leaving town after bedding a woman two feet taller than him & she's become attached. *shit happens*, he says. *go west.*

we've read about it: a pacific raw & squirming, mussels caking every surface, & the scales of fish translucent with a grand inhuman light. i still believe that pain is a suit you can leave behind. i want to bleach my guts of me. so witch-auk and i decide to go together: toward forgetting.

witch-auk takes one last dip in the atlantic, shoots beneath the waves, & the bent fish wriggle back to life as she goes. i look over the railing at my reflection to wave goodbye. we haven't seen each other in a long time. maybe someday she'll be worth saving.

The railing

Why did you leave?
To go west was to break in a way I needed breaking.

Where did you live?
I tunneled through the earth, hid in lime-crusted aquifers, stalactites lolling their sinuous tongues.

Why were you hiding?
I was godless. It was the third grade. This was revealed.

What happened then?
Nothing redeems the defect. It is made of me, like clay is made of earth. It's not the moment that hurts, but the moment after.

What did you learn?
You'll like what you see if you see what you like. So I hid for the rest of my life, The End.

Who else was in the cave?
The great auk—un-bird—un-belongs everywhere.

With whom did you travel west?
The auk's uncanny afterimage: witch-auk, who swims & performs magic.

What did you leave behind?
God I fled, god I left beheaded, and that defective girl—coming out the cave, I looked over my shoulder on purpose: to make her disappear.

What are you now?
Your reflection in glass. Do you like it?

Where did she go?

She tunnels beneath my feet—the ghost   the ghost   the ghost   the ghost   the ghost   the ghost
who knows I'm lying.

"On the Recrystallization of Fallen Snow"

After a paper read by John Wolley at a meeting
of Scandinavian naturalists, Christiania, Denmark, 1856

Spit of sail across the water, and I was in love. Tindhólmur
Isle like a broken jaw shoved up into a crash of gulls.

Waved into berth. We bagged cormorants right off the dock.
I've been where Saharan sand blows a thousand miles to land

on my eyelids. Here, even the roofs bloom. Wet-nosed deer
pick forever at their eaves. Each creature seems sewn

for its domain like a glove for fingers. Some tastes linger
on the tongue: those fallen flags of weather I melted

to drink all winter; blood hatched from my lips. I found
in a pine grove a wild swan's nest, the pair frozen in place,

all our bodies caked by the same storm. A whole Arctic winter
I passed in the dark, forgot if my eyes were shut or open. Between,

too, is somewhere. Tent-rows of glass mountains. Look:

witch-auk finds me hiding in the girls' bathroom, ca. 1995

witch-auk blears into being
where the steam meets the glass & the glass

dazes—
takes me by the wing—

clack-beak—faucets—
brisk streams, soap- pink twang—

then summons
the dryers' thaw:

hush hush
i know

hush hush
i know.

witch-auk i don't
belong to anything

& i am past trying.
the future concurs see it grinning

pleats of yellow
snarl.

but she presses me to her
feeds me live

sparks

from her own stomach.

o constellated creek
what tastes like love?

inside the egg, the chick
learns to swim. the rest

of my life, I gasp
between islands.

The dream, the static
(or, the researcher attempts to reach—)

Birch in the blue field.
Color of keepsake shooing
all round. No. Let the deer
softly. Tuft of billow hair.
At the fence and nudging
toward the spear. This: look:
the light revolves. Gap
and gap of the sea
as it moves. She is kept
in the palm of the earth
like a stone. Turns
little in her sleep. Let
the geese close. Sleep
is a type of lonely. No.
Again. Her sister's hands
folding sheets of bark:
scalloped pails, snowflake
cut-outs, canoes the size
of caught char. Not
to row. No. To remember.
She holds her breath. Squeezes
a mauve stone. She dreams
of paddling so far out
where no one she knows
has ever gone. She is lost
there. Then the geese come,
the auks and mallard
and cormorants, fold her
into themselves and she
is a new bird. No. Again.

They guide her to shore:
an island so undisturbed
that it quakes with song.
Standing on that beach
is the last time she'll be lonely.
She rows back to tell them.
Homing.

witch-auk visits shanawdithit after the researcher has failed to arrive

how many pendants has shanawdithit placed around the necks of her dead—carved like convoys to the next island with feathers & webbed feet? so when witch-auk spills into the room on a girder of light, she is one more guide, answering that calling. shanawdithit extends a palm. the captor has asked her to draw, again, her family smiling. a breeze lacing their open hair. *summer dress*, he writes, *of man, boy, girls*, presents her the empty page. once she drew her room, its square lock, & her wrist went shaky, like she was boxing herself inside that suffocating name. *man, boy, girls*—like these words contain them. witch-auk sighs, drowsy beneath her hand; shanawdithit will not lift it. The captor crosses out his words, writes *nancy is a bad girl*. sends her crayons hurtling across the floor, the red & black crests of long waves. witch-auk opens her small wings wide, wider, until they enclose shanawdithit completely, & she is transformed into a globe of feathers, dark & glossy, shadow of the sun & its ever companion, so water rolls off her & she fills with water, & we can search the globe over but we'll never know her face.

Exhibit B: Translation

1. Instrument

My face in the glass replaced the exhibit:
          sails raised in steed shapes,
bound east from America, soon
          to berth on that plumed
continent: that bird's stomach
          stuffed with its own fat. Familiar,
yes. Like and unlike, yes. I've fed
          meat to its monuments
in hushed tones. The auk, meanwhile,
          sheltered her egg as sailors built
a stockyard around her. Around *it*.
          For to make a body a product,
the first step is devaluation. "God
          made the innocence of so poor a creature,"
observed one colonist,
          "to become such an admirable instrument
for the sustenation of man." Before his eyes,
          hundreds of auks were herded down
gangplanks into the boats. Beside him,
          Mr. L— proposes a translation of *Beothuk*
to *the Good Night Indians*. I am not
          constructing a metaphor. The auk and the Beothuk
do not represent each other. This is
          the diagram for a machine. An inheritance
that feeds me daily. In a film
          at the settlement museum, a priest concludes,
"When she dies, she will go to heaven."
          Gale and these punched sails gasp

for the weight they carry. Steed saddled
and trussed to the plow, all along
its gutting. An animal is anything
with a fence built around it. A beastly
sleet now cauls it. I thought I saw
my reflection, odd twist to the mouth.
I sliced it out. It grew back.
I sliced it out.

2. Sustenation

Eat quick what will not keep:
one feat that makes the worthy

worthy: look, I stayed in a castle:
ate black pudding: a trick to keep

blood fresh: Feat the Second:
for who survives, deserves

salvation: plus, Ancestry.com
traces my descent from kings,

thus I arrived feeling not that I
belonged: that this belonged to me:

likewise did the English call it
Newfoundland, as though till they

arrived, it was vacant; so too
could they claim the last

Beothuk woman died of "consumption,
the fatal disease of *her* nation":

(my italics): for blood will flee
when given exit: so this ruined

fortress leaking rain: so this vein
of mine leaking pudding: so too

the drained body that fed it:
the latest being I've let die

for my maintenance: stuttering
heart after stuttering heart.

3. Creature

Fluttery little heart beating there on the white
tile floor of the Palace of Providence.

Ventricles pulping away and spits of blood;
puffs of small steam rise

from the still-warm organ. On the stained tile
the shape spreads,

crisply defined by a sheen off its curved edge.
Meanwhile, in a meeting of the American

Philosophical Society, Mr. A— G— argues
that the real translation of *Beothuk*

is *I am going home*. Fluttery little heart
lying there on the white stone,

a fresh sea lapping in, globules of foam left behind
beside it. They inch down the slope,

every glob for itself, the bubbles inside them pop-
popping so the foam becomes,

before it reaches ocean, not worth mentioning.
Recall that just 350 words

in the Beothuk language were recorded, yet Mr. G—
observes, "it is puzzling

that the Beothuk should have had no word of their own
for *alive*." As though all that has happened

was preordained—and this heart cannot travel back
through the slit-wide belly,

recongeal where the veins were severed, then glint like a sunset
while the gut is sewn shut around it. Nor the down

reattach, the quills reinsert into their follicles. Let us all
shrug in unison: Oh well. Fluttery

little heart in my palm, where it has been always. It has never
belonged to me, but if it stops it will.

we've seen the need for disguises

in the changing room at the goodwill, witch-auk
will not make a decision. we've tried a lacy holiday
apron, horn-rimmed glasses (no lenses), a bow tie,

some mary jane pumps that (i should have predicted)
she can't walk in without tripping, an egg-shaped
basket in which to carry—should she ever carry—

& of course a pointed halloween hat, although
she does not find this funny. in the end we leave
undisguised—which I know is a mistake.

who can see her beauty? out on the sidewalk
the passersby whistle & bump us, the cars slow
& honk, a skateboarder ogles mid-kickflip,

& the milkman in milk cap quits swinging his pail.
witch-auk stops in a puddle. she won't budge.
the ripples expand from her feet. the water crests

& crests like she's dropping through it. the world slows
around us as though viewed through syrup:
& reflected on their eyes' curved planes

we are warped beings, though witch-auk shrugs
so what if we are. we ride the puddle all the way
to the river &, as we pass, all the petrified faces

look like tarnished crystal, like chipped goblets
or pennanted soldiers lining the pitch of our parade.
we catch the current, we drift off, we feel them waving.

Uncanny valley

Sigurðr's daughter, like all children, is too young to seem fully human. Through the doorway he glimpses her doll gesture at a missing sun. Windmilling arms. Her mouth moves like a wrench turns a screw: in jerks. The sick he feels at the sight, like watching that auk squirm in his fist, beak snapping—sighing.

◁

In an argument over an automaton passed off as a beautiful girl, the Sandman escapes with the body and leaves the eyes behind. It is not the automaton that's uncanny, Freud insists, but "the idea of being robbed of one's eyes." Still, wouldn't it be lovely? To perform most essential functions, without all our soft parts?

◁

One hypothesis for what causes the uncanny valley, if it even exists: categorization ambiguity. If it is too hard to determine whether a thing is human, the result is a negative emotional valence. This is uncomfortable.

◁

A forest cracks in two under heavy wind. The robot has "multiple modes of movement (degrees of freedom)." Tendon shooting through the trees. We are sprigs off a single trunk, some combination of wood/wire/meat. Dolls with joints like cysts lifting up the skin, or wounds like fist-wide pleas for devotion. Where the eyes are in this forest is the question. And who is the original.

◁

Freud's list of things that are uncanny includes:

- epilepsy
- dismembered limbs
- a hand cut off at the wrist
- madness

◁

It was customary during the Renaissance to banish the sick, the mad, and the foreign from city centers. They were transported elsewhere by boatmen. Some traveled forever from town to town but were never let in. The walls, like a tyrant, insist upon their own reason. Like a tyrant, they seduce with comfort. The walls, like a tyrant, warp breath into classifications, into yes and no.

◁

Another hypothesis: perceptual mismatch—inconsistency in human-likeness: say, too-large eyes on a face. Or a bird with a human gait, that paced like what it was thinking could not be reduced.

◁

O dear who tender-steps like. O deer who dips its soft meat lips. Its or her lips meet the water. You know a thirst like this. O plea on spackled rock. Oopsed with shit but brightly kind. Bright the yawn-blue sky. O auk sighing.

◁

One study concluded that "mismatched face–voice pairs elicited higher eeriness." The auk's mottled vein thumps where it meets his:

o—o—o—o it says.

◁

Being robbed of one's eyes by having never had them. I saw a robot with skin pasted all over it. Its lips ooh-ed at tiny animals. Did its oils quicken?

◁

We cut a hole above the North Pole to relieve the pull of its Almighty weight. Clammy star-gagged space wafting in. Relief. Let it also take this recurring dream: Sigurðr watches a girl drowning. She kicks the water. Yes, she says, yes—but she's confused the word with its opposite. There's no maybe. That's why she won't make it.

witch-auk & me stop over in my hometown

louisville, 2020

i bear witch-auk within the trench
of my coat all the route down the ohio.
we come ashore on an island no one has claimed

beyond the blonde wrecks of barges,
their haw-mouths & greedy smells.
mud furrows on her webbed toes,

she leans down to look, falls,
& the clouds snarl open their
filed teeth & the teeth fall.

all the city spins up, red blear
of sirens, we flee in all directions,
streetlamps squeal like hot plastic

but the teeth just bounce a little
& settle down. they are soft
& helix, they are the wounds

not the bullets, the walls
of a heart. the city, meanwhile,
fires thirty-two rounds.

in jefferson square park
tears orbit the ring of drains.
they are slow movers.

they are slow movers.
like a great navel filling up
with rain, so that the clouds forget

some days what they are doing
& stop to watch.
witch-auk what have i done

but fill the river with canines
that mouthed how this was just a dream.
witch-auk says nothing,

squirms to stand back up.
her small wings tug
at just a little air.

it is enough to right her,
though the mud beneath her feet
slides her backwards into the ohio.

Exhibit C: Ootheca Wolleyana

After An Illustrated Catalogue of the Collection of Birds' Eggs
begun by the late John Wolley; additions by Alfred Newton

On a fresh-laid egg, the colors bleed. Fleck-
brown milk down the table's seams. Once
I saw a mammoth's tusk pearling along
a tatter of river in the far north. *Oranges*
and lemons, Say the bells of St. Clement's.
I've been told to wait until I've suffered
more to speak. But what if I've caused
suffering? *When will you pay me? Say*
the bells of Old Bailey. Nearly hatched
eggs need a large hole. Hook and lacerate
the embryo, then let it drain. *Here comes*
a candle to light you to bed. I was still
learning when a shell collapsed in my grip.
Two little steeples, a church with people.
An egg is all skin inside. *And here*
comes a chopper to chop off your head.
Little pin-stemmed feathers.
Chip chop chip chop. Fully formed eyes.

Torches

The Grotte Cosquer (Cosquer Cave), discovered in 1985 on the coast of Provence, contains sixty-five hand stencils and 177 animal paintings, including three great auks.

16,500 B.C.E., PROVENCE

Being vastly superior is
this the way to
ask the question, down to *Les
Pointes de la Voile*
caves, the hovels of bears,
a huddle of
blades

given: the human animal is
one more beast, is this the way to
Calanques: the Rocky Inlet,
riddled with
lions, hyenas, ibex,
mares, chalcedony
scattered at their painted feet.

1996 C.E., UNIVERSITY OF ST. ANDREWS, SCOTLAND

Observe: the superior temporal
sulcus, Latin for *furrow*,
creased like
plowing, implantation,
resembled those plains
where the oceans rose and
simpering glaciers
retreated northward
tilling seed rows. The hands
dropping seeds and the seeds
the first example—

sulcus of the rhesus macaque monkey—
or *depression*: appears
in human brains. *Depress* is a type of
sinking. The mind, before its taming,
broken up by copses of Scotch pine,
sought to consume those
mammals on their chalk hooves. They fled,
clearing the path
of their pursuers,
blooming. Easy to track. This is just
cause and effect.

2000 B.C.E, PORT AU CHOIX, NEWFOUNDLAND

Two hundred
to
one

beaks
sepulcher this
human body

1996 C.E., UNIVERSITY OF ST. ANDREWS, SCOTLAND

Observe: trained monkeys
by a green LED light
in a primate chair
neckhole and chinplate not un-
flattering

licking fruit-juice prizes
or fed weak saline, placed
in a plexiglass pillory,
like the ruff collar of the
Elizabethan. The superior

part of the temporal sulcus
that interprets facial expressions—
is sensitive to *movement*.
So if a ball suddenly moves:
repulsive, because there's no
causation

—one region of the brain
proves sensitive to *form*,
especially hand-object interaction.
if a hand has pushed it, it's not
sentience: the monkey brain seeks
like the human brain does.

Small, wet
alder and birch,
of which
charcoal
remains—

depressions bordered by
the fossilized pollen
have been recovered in Cosquer Cave
drawings: auk

1840 C.E., NORTHERN EUROPE

of maybe millions
more than none

—three, in fact,
is enough

2001 C.E., *NEUROREPORT* JOURNAL

Detection of the causal
understanding
occurs
in the visual system and
(in a *simple billiard-ball causality*)
even by accident:
to witness
is to change it. Maybe they
appear in your next painting:
on an empty plate.

relationship between events is fundamental for
what is happening in the world around us—which
according to the present study
is automatic
that is, the act of relating: to come upon,
just over the bluff—
a pastoral: three birds
scatter. Maybe you chase. Maybe they
star as the missing meal

16,500 B.C.E., PROVENCE

The height of
the ice caps
several thousand feet tall

the Quaternary cold
coating Eurasia
made the sea recede.

Driving south
the thousand
converged at the Provençal shelf
having lost
to the water.

on the heels of reindeer
auk flocks swam and
now submerged
three hundred and sixty feet
Here,

spaciously skulled Cro-Magnons,
in nassa shells and
canines—bonneted
for ceremony
in a cave they
would visit, collect lime and clay,
to ask forgiveness. Paintings
galloping. How did it happen, when
the negative space of their
hands—when it too became
absent.

whose dead were ornamented
deer teeth—atrophied
with their heads turned right
—also remembered prey
couldn't inhabit, but
leave behind silhouettes
stoic or horned and
humans replaced

their predator.

Uncanny valley

At a mission in what is now called San Fernando, California; including excerpts from a Russian otter hunter who witnessed the event. 1815.

the calf doddered on new
hooves soft like a child's skull

for three days before it died.

now beside a waft of new
milkweed that burst beneath

its body, escapees, enslaved

members of a tribe whose name
this witness didn't record, were

taken out to the open field.

priests and soldiers tied the mothers
to their children. skinned the calf.

the next day we saw some terrible things:

so goes the sacrament: first
invent the animal, then

destroy it.

why do you look for the living
among the dead? a priest recited.

a name too stained to read.

all around the body, the milkweed
arose like a resurrection,

saved nobody.

when we are found we will be fused

witch-auk is not in a hurry
                    though hurricanes
skitter on the gulf like
                    dogs along a kitchen floor.

just to make her drowsy
                    i've fed her more milk
than is good for her; tied
                    the leash beneath her beak.

now she keeps her eyes
                    sheathed, though i say look
this will make us famous,
                    just transform the storm

back to sea, she's stopped
                    looking. sometimes a shiver
rises out of her chest, blurs
                    to the tips of her wings,

the way a hot gust lurches
                    pain from nothing we can see.
what, after all, isn't past
                    saving? there are many ways

the world can end, & some
                    have already happened.
we mount a dune. tar zebras
                    the beach, & the blonde gob

of hurricane like a lion
                    over that horizon peeping.

i tug the tether, but when
    i look down the beach

to where a single claw lifts
    from the sea to test the sand
for tension, she hops
    to slice my arm with her beak.

the part in a curtain. that thin
    sheet of helium between the water
& any savior's feet.
    she steps out of the leash

& into my arms. witch-auk i'm sorry.
    i rub sand into my cheeks,
rub the nose & eyes off of me
    as the storm charges, a mane

of tin tarpon cresting before it,
    fuel & festoon for the beast.
though she is all that i have,
    witch-auk gets lonely.

The researcher (2020) writes to Shanawdithit (1829) regarding her drawing of the devil

Stained ice, the lake.
You draw his hand
and they are wet the same.

The moon bangs down
its hammer face its round pit
of musket its name

bloodied in his teeth.
He does not stop to learn
the word for anything

before he wads it
into his ravenous.
A body dangles from

his neck. He worships
its gutting, he is never
glutted, demands that you,

who are also dying,
draw maps of massacres—
that you draw the "explorer"—

you cringe to touch him
through the lead—
who murdered Nonosabasut,

kidnapped his partner, Demasduit,
and, when their baby died,
named her after the Virgin Mary.

He calls you Nancy, scrawls translations
on top of the land you've cut out
of the blank.

9 — 1 dead leaves 8. The only land
you can touch without his lawn
between, its sliced-down grass.

*7 — Nancy's uncle & his daughter
shot.* You draw your uncle fleeing,
his trousers torn away in the snow.

He did not look like this.
This is not how he moved.
You draw Demasduit

as she lifts one arm, revealing
her wing.
And as for Nancy,

the name slides off of you
like oil. Maybe you feed it
to the fleck and flame—

mamateek—a home
you keep in your mind.
I don't know this. I only

hope you can still
carry it: the warm
tang of milk, yellow yawns

of weather off the sea,
your skin against skin,
your palm cupping her chin

while her eyes watch
over your shoulder
for spring. It's coming.

Drawings by Shanawdithit, c. 1828

Self-portrait skinning twenty-three auks

A little rasp in its throat whittled the exhaling air. The auk laid down at last
and stayed there, its breath
so quiet I didn't know when
it gave way to a greater quiet.
It watched the mound of birds

shrink to the left of me, while the mound of skins and bones grew
to the right of me. I can show
you on my arm what we kept.
The bird—she—having come
to the end of swimming—

lifted the nictating membrane from each eye, saw all of this clearly.
Once my mother showed
me how, on a chicken's body—
how a cloud shifted over my eyes
and I thought that I never could.

But there is pain at every stage of becoming a woman. Or a woman
is anything used to pain.
I can show you how I tallied
the days on my thighs, the soles
of my feet, where the skin still

belongs to me. How when he came at me, tried to rip off my shirt, I kept
laughing, laughed even as I
called for help and no one
came. Two women sat outside
that room watching movies,

snug in the knowledge that you get what you have earned. I emerged
smiling. I knew right away
that it is better to bury
the word—cloister it like
a seed. A woman is someone

who can clean blood out of anything. I write this poem bleeding. I make you watch me
peel the fat from the skin,
I make you look directly at it.
I can see it, most of the time,
and not suffer. And I can tell you

the color of the eyes when the membrane lifted: hazel. But this is your mistake:
to think those were the real thing.
The fog, the haw—how she protected
herself against invasion, flooding.
Her eyes were the membrane.

Self-portrait as both auk and child

No no no no no, not the neck, not the lungs
below it, not the ankles or the whiff
of salt on her, not her white socks or leather
loafers, the feet inside strung with cuts.
For, consider: cuts that spring of themselves
could be stigmata, arisen from a *contemplated*
pain. No, just my skin peeling open,
hoping there is beauty on the bone.
And isn't it possible? Look how superbly long
His toes (cf. el Greco), their doe-shy flush.
Which is not to say she/I suffered
that much. She's hysteric: the few times
she swung a boyfriend, she puked out her nerves
every morning until she/I couldn't.
Not the throat, but the sour pit below it.
Rumination, a.k.a. excess thought,
leads to corrosion, cf. Jesus's take on
kindness, now summed up into a wad of spit
inside this nonbeliever's child-sized loafer.
So, too, the plash of blood out the auk's beak
as he/she was being choked/was choking:
it landed between index and thumb:
one more coupon for His Magic Kingdom.
And that she/I should run for cover
would not, were it bird/me, make us cowards.
It's instinct. O see, what self-starring
tragedies I've sewn from minor wounds.
Look again: we will not see a strangling—
a metaphoric crime, or a disturbing lie.
Rather, we'll see its squat body, oafish on land,
its chump wings, and call this a simple failure:
and where flight is only through air it is.

Uncanny valley

"Unheimlich [uncanny] is the name for everything that ought to have remained . . . hidden and secret and has become visible."
—Friedrich Wilhelm Joseph von Schelling

Sigurðr, like all sailors, had seen monsters. How the squirming whats flash their fins above the foam. How the seabirds moan and wail what cannot be song.

monstrum (Latin) Divine omen; abnormal shape.

And the masks that replaced the faces of the once-living: didn't they remind you of their living faces? It was after all their skin, their eyelashes, just some ineffable tension so ghastly gone. How the sailors who slipped and bashed their heads on the rocks, and drowned, would return in different shells that looked like the men they had been, but were not those men.

pupa (Latin) Girl, doll, puppet.

(English) Post-larval state of an insect.

So Sigurðr left his double on shore in the form of a straw doll for his daughter, which did not resemble him in height or the placement of his features. That way it could remind her of him, but should he come back drowned and slipped inside that top-sheet of same-skin but not-him, she should not find there the uncanny, the worst kind of haunting, but simply a stranger.

moneie- (Proto-Indo-European, root of *monster*) To remind, to make think of.

But when Sigurðr lifted that last auk by the neck, he saw in its dangling body the straw doll, which was supposed to resemble but not *be* human. The auk was not supposed to resemble but was resembling him. How it sighed in his fist, once, when it saw what he was doing. Like a child that tosses back into bad sleep.

pupil (English) Part of the eye; so named because, when one looks inside it, a tiny image of oneself is reflected back.

When Sigurðr held his daughter in his arms as a baby, he would sometimes become aware of the distance between the floor and her body, of the choice that he had to throw or not throw her down. This was power but it made him sick. He shoved it back down into the pocket where, he feared, he had always kept it.

unheimlich (German) Uncanny, meaning "not familiar."

One full day they rowed a sailor's body back to shore with plump auks tucked all around him, as though the hunger that had once been inside the sailor now clung to his outsides, dark berries that the other men could now pluck and consume.

animale (Latin) Living being; that which breathes.

The sailor's body was curled in upon itself like a caterpillar in its cocoon waiting. Sickness is a word for pardon, madness is a word for finding omens in everything. Sigurðr thought that he saw in the faces of the dead—the sailor, the auks beside him—his own face. Or that the masks they wore were some average of them all.

heimlich

II. Concealed, kept from sight.

[. . .]

(a) (Grimm's dictionary) Something withdrawn from the eyes of others.

When he was home, he would pluck stray straw from her doll to keep it clean and neat. Over time, the doll slimmed to a ghost of its own memory. That is, when he looked at it, he saw the doll as it used to be. He could only see it as it was in brief flashes.

anima (Latin) Soul; breath; current of air.

What he saw in the eyes of the bird in his fist was recognition: something in the panicked clasp of sailors out to sea and outside of law. How, in the absence of witness, he opened that same secret pocket close to his chest. Exhalation; vapor. When the auk's eyes drained of sense, he saw a monster—or a reflection.

Exhibit D: Funk Island, Newfoundland, 1863

European fishermen kept kettles burning on Funk Island, one of the largest great auk nesting sites, for nearly three hundred years, starting around 1534. Auks were thrown alive into the boiling water.

Molloy carried, for runny nose,
a book of poems: Whitman.
Those verses being irrelevant
to sailors, one man tore *Behold!*
This is the compost of billions
of premature corpses, from page
209. He wiped the tears
the wind ripped from his eyes.
Ten huddled days in a hut
of pink granite. Puffins watched
from a crumble of pens.
The crew rested on turf specked
with spoonwort like little mice
teeth. One rolled a cigarette, as
I understand it, using a page
that declared, *That when I recline*
on the grass I do not catch
any disease! and ended, *Now*
I am terrified at the Earth!
One dug his fists into the soil,
still felt eggshell a foot
deep. *It grows such sweet things*
out of such corruptions, said
the sheet in which they folded
one of three auk mummies.
At last, they shipped off for Saint John,

sold five tons of compost
at auction, nineteen dollars each.
The rest shipped to Boston,
where a child, in her garden, found
a feather beneath a plum tree.

During a pandemic, the researcher (2020) wonders about Shanawdithit's last year (1829)

at last the feathers sink
into your skin—heavy legs

molted—your body new and
sudden—and webs of light

climb down the water
to crown your head—you dart and dive

and surface—swallow bright
capelin—and new muscles

wrap around yours—guide you
west—to that happy island

where everyone waits—
then you wake on a mattress.

quills gnaw through the seams.
the house cat is purring

while she snaps the bones
of a sparrow into small bits.

you squirm with fever. the pillow
spits up feathers. they peak

in a mull of sun. suspend.
drop again, settle onto your fists, weave

into the hair on your arms and legs.
you shut your eyes. lashes hot

on your skin. the body can carry
so much death inside it. but the sea

is a promise: sustenance,
sustaining. us is the language it speaks.

Shovels down

Reader, I can't dig that water to the woods—I can't gut the pool that sustains her—so let them huddle in—the trunks the streaks of mottle snow and the needles waxed and fallow. And no, I do not know her, reader—I cannot. Nor can I want for her what waft of yellow light I do not know can comfort. She hasn't spoken to us—and if she has cast even a breath—she hasn't asked us to catch it. And so this is the ocean of know-not—and each poem is a failed companion. But sometimes I dream her through the wattle fence through the duck blind the brine maw—and reader, more so every year—I cannot wake and watch the weather sieve her down—I cannot wake and watch the water press the stone into itself as though it will not float—and it will not float. Reader, I want us to hold her. To loft her into the raft and fold of a small wave and let her go.

greatest

witch-auk & me sweat from our seams & sleep in our dreams & the trek has grown so exhausting that i don't recall the last truck or the truck

before it, just that they've been mack trucks and this too's a mack truck. witch-auk dangles her flippers over the stick shift

over rubber mats with bulldogs on them over the pinkish road rolled out over a hundred miles of colorado scrubland.

little use for flippers here. the driver starts the conversation with *where you headed*, like they all do.

he says he's bound home, points to a photo adhered to the dash of a woman with feathered bangs, her hands on the shoulders of a small girl.

i say witch-auk has relatives in california—the greatest auk, *miomancalla howardae* (though when I told her this,

she didn't want to hear). *had* relatives, i correct myself, many years ago. the driver laughs in a way that's not glad, says *i get it,*

nods at the picture, *she's older now* he says. witch-auk wants to ask how much older & i tell her that's enough & keep quiet.

the driver twists at his beard with one hand on the wheel. the radio crackles into silence & he gets to humming & witch-auk

starts clacking her beak in counterpoint—like she knows the tune. he clicks the headlights on & we drive through the night like this—that song in so many variations that i never can figure out how to join in. around four a.m., the driver starts crying, tears wriggling

down the wires of his beard. witch-auk leans against his arm. i have moved like a ghost across my own waking. through everyone i meet.

Guanahaní

The Ocean Sea's ever-churning,
churning, mixed mists with our steaming
breaths. See the bird
found dead on deck, whispers of down
at its throat. Piss overboard
and keep towing forward. Rip bones
from the sea, divest them
of meat, toss them over the railing.
Now we are conquerors.
Later, returning east, we will just
be sailors. But don't forget
how that bird landed on *our* ship,
genuflected at the might
of it, thanked whatever bird-god
to be ours. How,
when we made land, reflected
in the eyes of the men
and women and children, we did not
know ourselves.
Like they'd taken our places: frozen
at the turns a life takes
all outside of our control. Later, much
later, birds found dead
in droves will be called *wrecks.*
There will be so few
sailing ships, we'll use the word elsewhere
lest it go extinct. We,
meanwhile, will be thriving—not inside
our bodies, but
in the way the land curves, terrified,
into distance.

"Fallen Snow under intense Cold"

After a paper read by John Wolley at a meeting of the British Association, Leeds, 1858

Languorous summer. Glaciers parted like hair. A new
moon tunes the auroras brighter; they hiss electricity
out their spackling maws. My last night up north,
a red phalanx of light crossed the breeze. This fed
on such gluts of oxygen as I've never seen.
On a reindeer-trussed sledge, I traversed
the Kjølen range, on every lake a crust

of hexagonal cracked snow. The Sami dig this up
for their wash and kettles. My reindeer kicked
at loch-edge to scout nests of whitlow grass.
The crackle of their soft noses: I remember this.
But, Alfred—he has to remind me of the sealskin
boats lined up on Iceland's docks, the geysers
spewing sulfur as we waited for good weather.
We were to row out and see where the auk was not—
and never saw, if I remember. These days, the headaches

leave me breathless. I sketch sashes of light across
my books. I mull more on inheritance; cf., my paper,
"Observations on the Arrangement of small Stones."
But with winter's approach, I sense a speedy change

taking place, riches of oxygen, the end of devouring
this thin air, of gluttonous tall light, of warming
the reindeers' cheeks with my smoke. Should you need
to know, write *he expired without suffering.*
There is so much snow, one must either dig through it,
or lie down. This time, at least, let it be restful.

witch-auk & me reach the pacific

having spruced up our new
isle, plucked clear the beard
of its citadel, except for one

access—a basalt slope only
she & i know—witch-auk
snuggles down into a mound

of eelgrass & shells.
looks around herself.
like an egg is coming.

like it will arrive
from the outside, since
she has never in her life

seen how this works.
i have adorned
the slope's bannisters:

feather-tongued barnacles,
tassels of bull kelp,
its hollow knobs filled

with sludge that glows
when you shake them,
which the sea does & does.

this ocean is an ever-
exhaling; bright foam
spits high into the cedars,

& the salt tastes pink
or like bubbles scooping
out a cetacean skull.

witch-auk shuts her eyes.
the waves stall.
with the sea gone

to glass, there is a way
that the clouds churn
below the water's surface

that makes me understand
belief. i set out rowing,
search the whole sea.

the sun, paused in its
route, boils like a yolk.
i don't know how long

we go on like this.

The researcher (2021) dreams again of Shanawdithit (1825)

Then time stops moving.
Birds dangle like scars
on the skin. Every
gorge of air the killer
snores in his bed next
door to your servant's
quarters is the same
breath, gorged again.
The glittering sea
dead as coins. Once
you drew every face
you could remember,
but the killer folded
that page into his pocket.
He folded Demasduit
into muslin, left her
coffin for you to find
on the frozen lake.
You can still hear
the ice squeal and snap
beneath, it happens every
day. Now you draw
that lake, red
lines spilling from it
like the sides of clouds.
You try to expel
the suffering and keep
her—you can see
her now, trimming fish

for the smokehouse,
shifting her limbs
through familiar shapes.
While the killer sleeps
you go out to the yard,
strike two lumps of pyrite
and lower the flame
to a husk of gull down, wet
from your fist. Together,
you share that quiet.

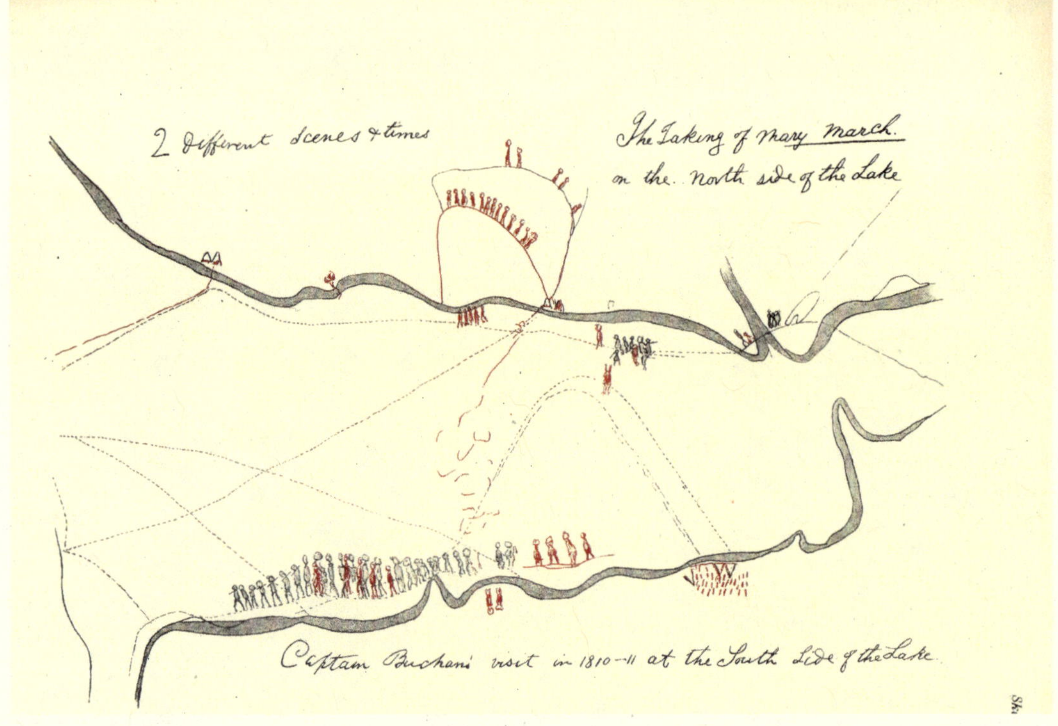

*Drawing by Shanawdithit**

* Reproduced without the permission of Alamy stock photos, which wanted $69.99.

Song alongside

The auk walks beside me up the hill.
I slow my pace for her. We weave

between the sidewalk's fissures,
its small quakes. It is spring,

cherry trees buttering a light wind.
Last night I drank so much poison

I broke the red arm of my glasses
like a little child. Saw my self

as I never see her, toddling
along the furred edge of Lake Eerie

like there was no end to that sound.
Unafraid, most of all, of herself,

how the taste on her lips shifted
as the lake lapped them. They were

beloved, parted like an egg's
burst of birth-sour & wet shining.

Who should we thank but water—
for how it poured out a bright

mirror below the egg to soften
the stone, for the way that I float

no matter how I try. Petal blown
to my cheek, the wet in both of us

holding, for we are mostly
the same thing, for how the ebb

where the auk is missing
will not let her shape go.

Evacuation of Hirta and the St. Kilda Islands

August 29, 1930

Those good storms, slick as braids on my neck. About Kilda,
mainlanders say there's no such saint,

just the Norse *sunt kelda*—sweet well water. Past the sheepfold,
a woman *much addicted to hunting*

built a house three hundred years ago. I found a helmet. *Hirtir*,
they say, for *stag*—but there are no deer

on these islands. Drenching storms by the hundreds; my skirt clung
whole days to my thighs.

When the tour yachts came, their leaflets called us dumb and guileless.
I sold them tweed. Placed it

in their festering hands. We were sick for the next twelve years.
Vomiting, weakness, blue skin

slinking up the cheeks. Babies curved like a Soay ram's horns
and locked to the shape.

When I got pregnant, he built me a coffin you could pile hay up in
to make a crib. Twelve years

and half of us left. In Celtic, *Hirta* means *death*. We left a Bible
and a fistful of oats in each house.

We drowned our dogs in the sea. All the way down to the boat
I fed the field mice barley,

stopped to lower it to their small mouths. What
will happen to them?

Someone told me that hunting began as self-defense. Here
there are no lions, so how

could we have learned? For this reason, I choose another
Celtic word, where *Hirta*

means the hope for distance. What it means is *west.*

witch-auk visits shanawdithit in lieu of april

between the falling flakes of a late-winter snow, witch-auk shudders into view. shanawdithit, still small enough to be unsteady, toddles forward to pinch the feathers on her belly. the bird tilts her head. shanawdithit's father says witch-auk reminds him of when his grandfather would row a thousand strokes past the fog to a lone crag so swarmed with auks that he could chase whole flocks into the boat. the flightless birds would tumble straight into his arms. eggs boiled, dried, & powdered for broths, fat to stoke the fires. now are slimmer winters. the children's bones grow in stops & starts. witch-auk lifts her beak, spits up into the air a ream of seal skin so lustrous that it cracks the light. the skin rises to just below the clouds then pours out & down like a dome—down into the trees & with a great crunching shatters the frozen soil, sinks into the fissures & seals off the encampment from everything around. a quiet; the blood in their ears thumping. sun shivers through the speckled hide. shanawdithit grips witch-auk's feathers, chews her tongue with her few teeth. witch-auk lies down. witch-auk stops breathing. i remember this, says doodebewshet, cradles her up & takes her into the smoke.

"Memoir of the late John Wolley," by Alfred Newton

The Carrington Event was a spectacular aurora-related occurrence that created northern lights around the world in late August and early September, 1859. John Wolley died on November 20 of that year. Ootheca Wolleyana, *Wolley's magnum opus, was published in its final form nearly fifty years later. It was edited by Alfred Newton.*

By that premature end, John forgot
even our walks along Cape Reykjanes, net sacks on our arms,
whole fogged days
spent collecting auk bones. Beaks light as leaves clumped
where the eddies left them.
One rib I lifted to examine snapped off in a heavy breeze. John
bagged it, said Don't worry, said Nothing
you could have done. Eldey Island, tea table perched on the horizon,
may as well have been set
with empty plates. In his last year, John's letters wore the wrong dates;
he wrote that we should sail to Iceland,
when we'd already gone. An attack of the brain left him bedridden,
a pool of sweat cupped
in his hands. He would study any ocean you gave him.
Once, before dawn, the sky
caught fire. I took his arm and we went outside. Too far south,
emerald northern lights crowned
the National Gallery dome. I learned later a telegraph operator in Boston
talked for two hours without battery
to Portland—just the air's charge powering this. I need to say I kept warm
every slip of paper he ever touched.
Though every time I sat down to write the book, all I could see
was that room where we slept:
the sealskin rotting from its drums, the stars black while towers
of cloud groaned. I wish

there were the slightest chance. But until I write that every auk is dead, it won't
have happened.
John leaned on my arm. The gaslights were off all down the street.
The aurora scrawled
long sleds of ink, as though the North itself had come to call on him.
I must let the birds live,
I'm sorry. Beneath the northern lights, John said, I believed I'd seen the last
of them. They had to escape
to a new ocean, but they survived. He said, Perhaps, I also will.

post-pacific

look, witch-auk, whoever has ever
owned the whole sea, has made it tiny.

shallow in its skins of oil & cups.
slug-tongued with sunk hulls &

the drug of smearing warmth.
who has owned the whole sea

think they too own us—but they don't,
do they? not the cotton-stuffed body of [ ],

killed on eldey & propped on a plank
in a brussels museum. not the body of [ ]

out for cleaning at the smithsonian.
instead they showed me a shoebox of bones.

i didn't want to tell you, but there's nothing in me
you can't reach. not the felt of new snow

that told me one winter to stop trying.
not that lunchroom table where i said too much

& never will again. not the bottle of cognac
a man whose name i've forgotten

brought to my door, & i let him
like i was a machine. but he doesn't

have me. do you understand? nor
the ocean, whatever he calls it.

nor does the egg you never laid
deliver back into his grip. if you & i

came out not-quite-human, came out
monstrous, i still love the careful way

you nudge a blade of bull kelp
washed ashore in this last world

twisted to the shape of that last world.
this is ours—our disappointment.

also ours: how you place me whole
into the palm of my own hand.

On swimming

Dearest but also, who can survive in too
sadness. It sinks you like a lead plumb. Dear

and also gone, chick departed, yet another,
yes. But quiet. See how the sky closes

all its doors, its sudden moods, shields us
from the gasp. What goes on in space?

Spackles of night-bright plankton
regurgitated up, instead of down into a chick's

stomach. It taunts there forever, dangling
luminescence, nosing after the night's

constant pace. Each summer brings a spate
of eggs, set to rolling by the wind in wide arcs

too close to shore. The ocean cares very much,
wherever those go. Some chicks sink over-stuffed

with sculpin. Others starve. Some are netted up
by boats, and if dusk or the night comes, rise

toward those plankton, past the clouds, maybe
to a new sea. Their bodies shift

before they know. This is only flocking—now
through the destitute air, thin as it is and fishless,

frail as it is with just one meal inside it.
Best to call this a lesser kind of flight.

NOTES

"Exhibit A: Eldey Island, Iceland, 1844"

Quotations from crew members were recorded by John Wolley on a trip to Iceland in 1858 and published by Alfred Newton in *Ibis* (1861).

"Occurrence of a Foreign Bat in Orkney"

All poems featuring John Wolley bear titles from papers or the book that he wrote.

"auk in the afterlife"

Please note that witch-auk is not the great auk. She is an afterimage of the auk in St. Kilda, an anthropomorphic projection with the aim to blur the line between the human and nonhuman such that the categories begin to reveal themselves for the constructions that they are. After this first appearance, witch-auk will perform an act of magic in every poem.

"The researcher (2020) dreams of Shanawdithit (1828)"

Shanawdithit was likely one of the last surviving members of Beothuk people. The Beothuk were hunter-gatherers who painted their bodies, faces, and belongings with red ochre; used birchbark for a wide variety of applications, from canoes to vessels for food; and buried their dead in caves and overlooks facing the sea. They traveled to Funk Island in the summers to gather great auks and their eggs for food.

The Beothuk were systematically denied access to coastal areas by European settlers and often clashed with colonists. This genocidal campaign lasted several hundred years until the last of them were wiped out.

Shanawdithit was instantly fascinated with drawing, and took to it with great skill. Her mother, Doodebewshet, and sister, whose name was not recorded, died of tuberculosis. Shanawdithit spent the next several years living with European colonists. During this time, she aided in documenting some 350 words of the Beothuk language, and drew pictures depicting the Beothuk culture and lifestyle as well as some of the traumatic events she had witnessed, including the murder of her uncle, Nonosabasut, by an expedition of colonists led by John Peyton, Jr. Shanawdithit later worked as a servant for five years in Peyton's household. (Peyton is "the killer" referred to in "The researcher (2021) dreams again of Shanawdithit (1825).") She died of tuberculosis in 1829, at around the age of twenty-nine.

An article published by Todd J. Kristensen and Donald H. Holly in the *Cambridge Archaeological Journal* in 2013 proposes that seabirds were a central part of Beothuk spirituality and may have been looked to as guides to help the dead travel to an island after death. This island lay to the west.

Thank you to Karen LeDrew-Day of the Beothuk Interpretation Centre for aiding me in this research.

Drawings by Shanawdithit

During the last year of her life, Shanawdithit lived with William Eppes Cormack, whose annotations are seen on many of her drawings.

"post-atlantic"

All credit for the slogan, "Shit happens. Go west," belongs to a man I met in Port Townsend, Washington. His name was Gary.

"Uncanny valley [Sigurðr's daughter]"

Sigurðr, who killed one of the last two known great auks, experienced a slippage of pronouns at the recollection: "It walked like a man. . . . He made no cry." This poem is in conversation with "The Sandman" (E. T. A. Hoffmann, 1816) and "A review of empirical evidence on different uncanny valley hypotheses" (Jari Kätsyri et al., 2015).

"Exhibit C:* Ootheca Wolleyana*"

The italicized lines are from "Oranges and Lemons," a seventeenth-century nursery rhyme that was still somewhat well known during Wolley's lifetime.

"Torches"

Some of the italicized quotations in this poem come from scientific studies published in *NeuroReport* and *American Physiological Society.*

"Uncanny Valley (the calf . . .)"

All quotes but one are from the narrative of Vassili Petrovitch Tarakanoff, a Russian who traveled with a group of Aleut Indians to California to hunt sea otters. There, they were captured by the Spanish. "Why do you look for the living among the dead?" is from Luke 24:5, and precedes the lines, "He is not here; he has risen!"

"The researcher (2020) writes to Shanawdithit (1829) regarding her drawing of the devil"

"[A]nd yet it is precisely because he did show that he possessed feelings common to us all . . . that he was shot." —Surveyor General Joseph Noad, on the murder of Nonosabasut, who died trying to protect Demasduit

"Self-portrait skinning twenty-three auks"

This poem was inspired in part by the story told by Icelandic fishwife Sigríður Thorláksdótter, who has provided some of the only testimony as to the color of the great auk's eyes. She learned this when preparing twenty-three killed auks in 1831. She saw one of them alive and said that the bird's eyes were hazel.

Some of Thorláksdótter's words are paraphrased in the poem.

"Exhibit D: Funk Island, Newfoundland, 1863"

A pre-1863 edition of *Leaves of Grass* is quoted in the poem, as cited below; statements in this poem about where particular lines appear on the page are not accurate, however. Thanks to Theresa Mudrock, University of Washington Libraries, and Deborah Andrews, Centre for Newfoundland Studies, for helping me track down information on the Thomas Molloy expedition to Funk Island in 1863–1864.

"Fallen Snow under intense Cold"

A few clusters of words in this poem are quoted or paraphrased from the writings of John Wolley and Alfred Newton. For instance, after an "attack" in July of 1859, several months before his death, Newton writes that the doctor "at once declared that the case was one in which no hope of recovery could be entertained, that there was an affection of the brain, probably of long standing, and that a speedy change would take place."

"'Memoir of the late John Wolley,' by Alfred Newton"

John Wolley died in 1859 without having published a complete catalog of his research. His friend, Alfred Newton, did not complete the publication of this work until 1905. He called it *Ootheca Wolleyana*, which translates roughly to "Wolley's egg catalog."

BIBLIOGRAPHY

Anonymous. "Sketches of the Savage Life." *Fraser's Magazine for Town and Country* 13, 75 (March 1836): 316–323. http://www.mun.ca/rels/native/beothuk/mcgregor.html.

Beebe, Rose Marie, and Robert M. Senkewicz. *Lands of Promise and Despair: Chronicles of Early California, 1535–1846.* Santa Clara, CA: Heyday Books, 2001.

Bendire, Charles. *Directions for Collecting, Preparing, and Preserving Birds' Eggs and Nests.* Washington, DC: Government Printing Office, 1891.

Bennett, Gabriella. "St. Kilda's daily diet: 36 eggs and 18 seabirds." *The Times*, Dec. 29, 2016, https://www.thetimes.co.uk/article/st-kilda-s-daily-diet-36-eggs-and-18-seabirds-gc37tlbjm.

Blakemore, Sarah-Jayne, Pierre Fonlupt, Mathilde Pachot-Clouard, Céline Darmon, Pascal Boyer, Andrew N. Meltzoff, Christoph Segebarth, and Jean Decety. "How the Brain Perceives Causality: An Event-Related FMRI Study." *NeuroReport* 12, no. 17 (2001): 3741–3746.

Bodkin, Henry. "Plot hatched to reintroduce extinct great auk to British shores." *Telegraph*, Aug. 19, 2016, http://www.telegraph.co.uk/science/2016/08/19/plot-hatched-to-reintroduce-extinct-great-auk-to-british-shores.

Clottes, Jean and Jean Courtin. *The Cave Beneath the Sea: Paleolithic Images at Cosquer*. New York: H. N. Abrams, 1996.

Cramb, Auslan. "Photograph of sea eagle carrying lamb reignites row over Britain's biggest bird of prey." *Telegraph*, May 9, 2017, http://www.telegraph.co.uk/news/2017/05/09/photograph-sea-eagle-carrying-lamb-reignites-row-britains-biggest.

Dawson, Ashley. "Biocapitalism and De-extinction." *After Extinction*. Richard Grusin, editor. University of Minnesota Press, 2018.

Forestry Commission England. "White-tailed eagle." https://www.forestry.gov.uk/forestry/white-tailedeagle.

Foucault, Michel. *History of Madness*. Translated by Jonathan Murphy and Jean Khalfa. Abingdon-on-Thames, UK: Routledge, 2009.

Freud, Sigmund. "The 'Uncanny.'" Translated by Alix Strachey. *Sammlung*, 1919.

Fuller, Errol. *The Great Auk.* New York: Abrams, 1999.

Gaskell, Jeremy. *Who Killed the Great Auk?* Oxford, UK: Oxford University Press, 2000.

Gill, William Wyatt, and Smith, Stephenson Percy. *Rarotonga Records: Being Extracts from the Papers of the Late Rev. W. Wyatt Gill.* New Zealand Society, 1916.

Higgins, Charlotte. "St Kilda's haunting story is retold in Edinburgh." *The Guardian*, Aug. 14, 2009, https://www.theguardian.com/stage/2009/aug/14/st-kilda-island-birdmen-edinburgh.

Hogenboom, Melissa. "Why are we the only human species still alive?" *BBC*, Sept. 29, 2015, http://www.bbc.com/earth/story/20150929-why-are-we-the-only-human-species-still-alive.

Howell, Frederick W. W. *Icelandic Pictures Drawn with Pen and Pencil.* United Kingdom, Religious Tract Society, 1893.

Howley, James P. *The Beothucks, or Red Indians: the Aboriginal Inhabitants, of Newfoundland*. Cambridge, UK: Cambridge University Press, 1915.

Kätsyri, Jari, Förger Klaus, Mäkäräinen Meeri, and Takala Tapio. "A review of empirical evidence on different uncanny valley hypotheses: support for perceptual mismatch as one road to the valley of eeriness." *Frontiers in Psychology* 6 (2015).

Kristensen, Todd J., and Donald H. Holly, Jr. "Birds, Burials and Sacred Cosmology of the Indigenous Beothuk of Newfoundland, Canada." *Cambridge Archaeological Journal* 23, no. 1 (February 2013): 41–53.

Lucas, Frederic A. *The Expedition to the Funk Island, with Observations upon the History and Anatomy of the Great Auk.* Washington, DC: Government Publishing Office, 1890.

Marshall, Ingeborg. *A History and Ethnography of the Beothuk.* Montréal: McGill-Queen's University Press, 1996.

———. "Belief-Related Beothuk Practices." Beothuk Institute; Newfoundland and Labrador Heritage website. Last modified February 2012. http://www.heritage.nf.ca/articles/aboriginal/beothuk-beliefs.php.

———. "Beothuk Language." Beothuk Institute; Newfoundland and Labrador Heritage Website. Last modified Feb. 2012. http://www.heritage.nf.ca/articles/aboriginal/beothuk-language.php.

———. "Disappearance of the Beothuk." Beothuk Institute; Newfoundland and Labrador Heritage Website. Last modified Feb. 2012. http://www.heritage.nf.ca/articles/aboriginal/beothuk-disappearance.php.

———. "Hunting Tools and Techniques; Food Preparation and Storage." Beothuk Institute; Newfoundland and Labrador Heritage Website. Last modified Feb. 2012. http://www.heritage.nf.ca/articles/aboriginal/beothuk-hunting.php.

———. "Personal Appearance and Items of Clothing." Beothuk Institute; Newfoundland and Labrador Heritage Website. Last modified Feb. 2012. http://www.heritage.nf.ca/articles/aboriginal/beothuk-clothing.php.

Martin, Martin. *A Late Voyage to St. Kilda*. 1698 edition republished in *Undiscovered Scotland*. http://www.undiscoveredscotland.co.uk/usebooks/martin-stkilda/chapter01.html.

Newton, Alfred. "The Gare-fowl and its Historians." *Natural History Review* 18 (1865): 467–488.

———. *Memoir of the late John Wolley, Jun., Esq., M.A., F.Z.S., &c., &c.* London: Taylor and Francis, 1860.

Oram, M. W., and D. I. Perrett. "Integration of form and motion in the anterior superior temporal polysensory area (STPa) of the macaque monkey." *American Physiological Society* 76, no. 1 (1996): 109–129.

Pastore, Ralph T. "The Beothuk." Newfoundland and Labrador Heritage Website. Last modified Feb. 2012. https://www.heritage.nf.ca/articles/indigenous/beothuk.php.

Rein, Lisa. "Mystery of Va.'s First Slaves Is Unlocked 400 Years Later." *Washington Post*, September 3, 2006. https://www.washingtonpost.com/archive/politics/2006/09/03/mystery-of-vas-first-slaves-is-unlocked-400-years-later/7015c871-aabd-4ba2-b5ce-7c0955aa0d75.

Revive & Restore. "Passenger Pigeon Project." http://reviverestore.org/about-the-passenger-pigeon.

Whitman, Walt. *Leaves of Grass.* Boston: Thayer and Eldridge, 1860–1861, https://whitmanarchive.org/item/ppp.01500.

Wolley, John, and Alfred Newton. *Ootheca Wolleyana: An Illustrated Catalogue of the Collection of Birds' Eggs, Volume II.* London: R. H. Porter, 1864–1907.

Wyatt Gill, William. *Rarotonga Records: Being Extracts from the Papers of the Late Rev. W. Wyatt Gill.* New Plymouth: Reprinted from the *Journal of the Polynesian Society* by Thomas Avery, 1916.

Volcano World. "Volcano Folklore." *Oregon State University*. http://volcano.oregonstate.edu/book/export/html/1015.

Zimmer, Carl. "Bringing Them Back to Life." *National Geographic*, April 2013, http://www.nationalgeographic.com/magazine/2013/04/species-revival-bringing-back-extinct-animals.

ACKNOWLEDGMENTS

All my awe and infinite gratitude to my first writing group, the Tygrrs, brilliant minds and brilliant friends. E. Briskin, Brent Schaeffer, Billie Swift, and my personal hero, Amanda Baker: I will never be able to thank you enough. This book would not be what it is without you.

A million thanks to my writing group, Erin Marie Lynch, Gabrielle Bates, and Patrycja Humienik, for pushing these poems to be their strongest selves.

To my cohort and professors at the University of Washington MFA program, thank you for helping me grow beyond what I knew was possible. Linda Bierds, your belief in me kept me going when nothing else did. Thank you to Pimone Triplett, Andrew Feld, and Richard Kenney for your insight, your deep knowledge, and your mentorship. To my cohorts, for your fellowship and feedback: Rachel Edelman, Ainsley Kelly, Abi Pollokoff, Patrick Milian, Meagan Arthur, Kristin Gulotta, Michelle Anderson, Sarah Destin, Maria Mills, Catherine Bresner, Garrett Evans, and Will Durham. Thank you, Amy Balliett, for your support during my time in the MFA.

For your important work and gorgeous souls, Knox Gardner and Victor Chudnovsky—Buenos Aires forever.

What an honor to learn with and from you, Joy Priest, Kary Wayson, francine j. harris, Martha Serpas, Ryan Bollenbach, Ana M. Gómez-Bravo, Anthony Geist, Cary Wolfe, Ashley Warner, Aris Kian, Inma Raneda-Cuartero, José Francisco Robles, and Suzanne Petersen.

To the Noemi team: thank you, thank you, thank you for believing in and supporting this book, for your insightful feedback, and for bringing *Wrecks* into the world at last: Diana Arterian, Sarah Gzemski, Mariah Bosch, Suzi F. Garcia, Anthony Cody, and Alban Fischer. I am forever grateful to you.

Many thanks to the following publications and editors for publishing earlier versions of these poems:

A Dozen Nothing, "Occurrence of a Foreign Bat in Orkney", "post-atlantic", "we've seen the need for disguises", "greatest", "witch-auk & me reach the pacific," and "post-pacific."

Beloit Poetry Journal, "'On the Recrystallization of Fallen Snow.'"

Bennington Review, "Torches."

COAST | NoCOAST, "Evacuation of Hirta and the St. Kilda Islands."

The Nature of Our Times: Poems on America's Lands, Waters, Wildlife, and Other Natural Wonders, Poets for Science, print anthology: "auk in the afterlife"; digital anthology: "Exhibit D: Funk Island, Newfoundland, 1863," "Guanahaní," and "Song alongside."

Nimrod International Journal of Prose and Poetry, "'Notice of an Ice-carried Boulder at Borgholm'" and "'Memoir of the late John Wolley,' by Alfred Newton."

Once a City Said: A Louisville Poets' Anthology (Sarabande Books, 2023), ed. Joy Priest, "witch-auk & me stop over in my hometown."

Poet Lore, "auk in the afterlife," selected by Tarfia Faizullah for a "Surrealism and Strangeness" folio.

Seventh Wave, "Exhibit D: Translation," "Uncanny valley [Sigurðr's daughter . . .]", and "Self-portrait skinning twenty-three auks."

Virginia Quarterly Review, "Uncanny Valley [Pink millions . . .]," "The researcher (2020) dreams of Shanawdithit (1828)," "Exhibit A: Eldey Island, Iceland, 1844."

West Branch, "when we are found we will be fused," selected by Joy Priest for a special feature.

Thank you to my father, Doug: for making me an environmentalist, and for teaching me about the great auk. To my mother, Paula: for supporting my writing from the very beginning, and for reading me "The Raven" as a bedtime story. To my sister, Maureen: for being the kindest, most generous human being I've ever met.

To the love of my life, Anthony: thank you for every day.

PHOTO: BROOKE HERHERT

ERIN L. MCCOY's poetry collection, *Wrecks*, was a finalist for the Noemi Book Award. Her debut novel, *Underlake*, will be published by Doubleday in 2026. Erin's poetry and fiction have appeared in the *American Poetry Review*, *Best New Poets*, *Pleiades*, *Narrative*, *Conjunctions*, and other publications, and she was a finalist for the *Missouri Review*'s Miller Audio Prize. She holds an MFA in creative writing and an MA in Spanish and Latin American literature from the University of Washington.